On My Way To Find Christmas

By Joan Surace

Once upon a time, in a habitat near the water, there lived a zebra who was unlike the rest. She stood out from her family and the other zebras because her coat frequently changed into different patterns of unique stripes—a striking combination of red and white, green and black, and other vibrant colors. Her tail and ears were a vivid green, perfectly complementing her black nose.

Despite her colorful appearance, the other zebras distanced themselves from her, labeling her as an outsider and even going so far as to call her a "demon from outer space." The harsh judgments didn't deter her mother, Hope, from loving her dearly.

The challenges didn't end there. The zebra, adorned in her distinct colors, faced rejection from other animals in the habitat. The elephants and various creatures were wary of her, considering her an oddity. Still, the zebra, named Hope after her loving mother, faced each day with resilience, embracing her uniqueness amidst the challenges of acceptance.

In solitude, one day, Hope found herself strolling alone, pausing near a puddle of water. As she gazed at her reflection, she questioned,

Who am I?

Why does everyone despise me?

Do I carry some unseen affliction?

To her surprise, the water responded,

You're not a demon; you're merely different.

Your uniqueness serves a purpose, and you must believe in that.

7

Hope dismissed the voices, thinking

No, no, this must be hallucination.

I must be losing my mind.

Yet, the water persisted,

You're not crazy.

You must discover your own path.

What path? How will I know?

When the time comes, you'll recognize it.

8

As the water's voice faded, Hope pleaded,

"Wait, please tell me more! I'm lost and confused. What am I supposed to do now?"

With a nonchalant demeanor, the bird descended from the branch and inquired,

Hope, surprised by the talking macaw, turned around and asked,

Hey, stripy, what's happening?

Are you talking to me?

The bird responded sarcastically, "Well, I don't see anyone else here, so I guess it's you."

Muttering to herself, Hope thought,

I'm not the only one. I must be crazy.

Trying to dismiss the macaw, she continued walking, but the persistent bird insisted,

12

Hey, hold on. Did I offend you?

Turning around, Hope expressed her need for solitude, "I don't have time for this. I need to be left alone. Please, go away." Undeterred, the bird declared, "Hey stripy, I don't know what you're going through, but I'm coming with you."

Annoyed, Hope asked, Why do you have to be so annoying?

By the way, my name is Hope.

What's your name?

The bird, revealing its lonely past, replied

Oh, well! Now we are talking.

I don't have a name.

14

urprised, Hope asked,

Your mother didn't give you a name?

The bird explained, "Hey, I grew up alone in the habitat and found my own way to survive." Feeling sympathy for the bird, Hope offered, "Can I give you a name?"

Overjoyed, the bird eagerly agreed

"I would love that! But make sure it's a good one."

Hope, suggested,

Hmmm, how about Annoying?

The bird, not expecting that protested, "Oh no, why? Can you pick another name?" Laughing, Hope insisted,

No, that fits right in. You know exactly what I mean.

16

Quickly Annoying turns around, pauses in confusion, and looks at Hope.

Huh did your coat changes color, or it's just my imagination?

Ha! I think it's your imagination.

17

She then continues walking.

Suddenly, the wind intensified, and Annoying exclaimed, "We better move fast! A storm is on its way. Come on, let's go! No time to waste. See that floating island? Jump! Trust me, please!"

Hope, hesitating for a moment, looked at Annoying and said, "I guess I have no other choice." Annoying reassured her, "We don't have a choice. You jump; I fly."

19

In an instant, they found themselves on the floating island. As the temperature dropped, the wind started blowing fiercely, propelling them towards the ocean. In the middle of the commotion, they noticed a deer struggling to save a baby bear stuck on a tree branch and red flamingos atop a log, unable to reach safety.

Hope sprang into action, assisting the baby bear onto the floating island, while Annoying helped the stork escape the branch. The flamingos perched on the log faced a similar challenge. After a few struggles, everyone was safely on the floating island.

22

As the island took an unexpected turn towards the North Pole, panic set in. The inhabitants feared the cold and the harsh conditions, questioning where they were headed.

"Oh no, where are we going now? We can't go there; it's too cold. We'll never survive,"

Hope, speaking in a soft voice, reflected,

Maybe this is my journey.

All the animals stood still, listening intently to Hope's words. Then, turning around, she asked

Did you hear me talking?

"Yes, of course, we heard you."

NORTH POLE

Annoying interjected, "Okay, we need to stay focused and calm down. I'd like to share something with you all. I once made a wish that I would love to see Christmas, and maybe this is it."

However, the other inhabitants of the floating island, except Hope, reacted with disbelief. "Oh no, it's crazy. We know you! We need to get off this island now!"

25

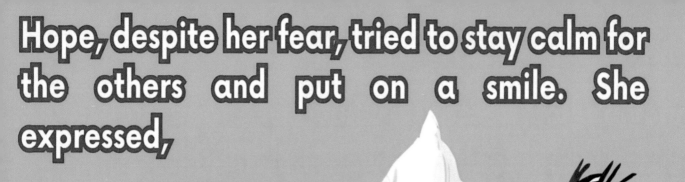

Hope, despite her fear, tried to stay calm for the others and put on a smile. She expressed,

I think it's wonderful. I would love to see Christmas. What about you all? Come on, let's do it.

Christmas is beautiful; it brings joy and hope into our lives. Let's take a chance.

Come on, we have nothing to lose on this floating island. Who is with me? Give me a big 'yes' if you agree.

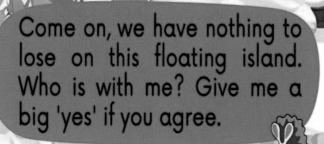

26

he stork was the first to respond, saying,

We don't have a choice. It's a yes for me.

he deer and the baby bear also expressed their agreement, and even the initially scared lamingos reluctantly admitted,

I guess we don't have a choice.

The flamingo and the stork flew away to help push the island, while everyone else cheered as they got closer.

Two Elves boarded the big island, and everyone surrounded them to keep warm.

Shivering, the Elves shared their story of losing their magic ones and falling into the deep, feeling homeless but never losing hope.

The first Elf asked,

May I ask where are you going?

We all want to see Christmas.

We're trying to get to the North Pole!

That's where we're going, but we don't have magic.

But do you know the way to get there?

Excitement filled the air as everyone eagerly exclaimed, "Yeah! Yeah! Let's go!"

Everyone exchanged their names, at least for now.

You're going to love it there!

It's beautiful, with snow everywhere and decorations of lights.

As far as your eyes can see, we have a factory with a built-in toy shop

and you're going to meet Santa Claus.

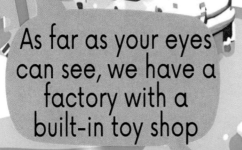

33

Annoying couldn't contain his excitement,

Oh yes, that's my dream.

I want to see Santa Claus, and then I'm going to sing!

Before he could finish his sentence, the stork interrupted,

Okay, okay, we got that. Let's get there first.

34

Everyone was now eager to see Santa Claus, and although the journey was a little rough, as soon as they arrived, they were greeted by Santa Claus and the rest of the elves. They couldn't believe their eyes a beautiful, enchanted Christmas wonderland. Christmas music filled the air, and Annoying couldn't contain himself.

36

Santa Claus graciously gave the elves back their magic, and they proceeded to show everyone around, revealing the beauty of the place. They all sat together at a big, round table, enjoying warm food and desserts, giggling, laughing, and singing joyous tunes.

Baby bear was delighted to meet his cousins, the polar bears, and had the time of his life playing in the snow building snowmen and chasing each other. Meanwhile, Santa Claus, along with the elves, Hope, Annoying, and the deer, worked tirelessly to fill the sleigh with toys to deliver to children around the world.

Words seemed to escape her, and she started to stutter

How do you know about me?"

I know everything."

So, do you want to change your coat?

It's just the way it is

I was born this way, so I'll stay like this."

You're very brave.

Santa nodded and smiled

42

Just then, a bunny called an Alpine Hare hopped by. Its white fur blended almost perfectly with the snow, except for the black insides of its ears, which stood out gently against the snowy backdrop

Santa chuckled and pointed to the bunny.

Did you know that winter bunnies are special too?"

In winter, their fur changes from gray to white to help them hide, and their coats keep them warm,"

The bunny, named Flurry, hopped over and said

Hello, I'm Flurry!

Hello, my name is Hope, but they call me Christmas. Your ears are so cool with the black inside!

Hope smiled as she watched the bunny hop away. She felt a little braver now. If the bunny could stay true to itself and still thrive in the winter, so could she. Santa leaned closer and whispered,

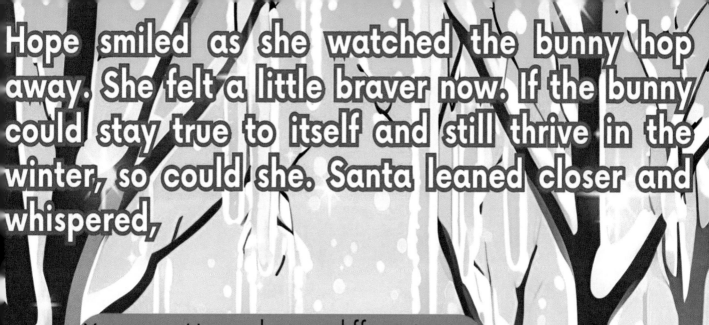

You see, Hope, being different is a gift. It makes you unique, just like that bunny's coat

Hope's heart filled with warmth, and for the first time, she felt proud of her coat.

As they prepared to leave, Flurry said excitedly "Can I come too?" he asked, hopping in circles. Santa chuckled. "Of course, Flurry! There's always room for a helping paw.

But soon, they realized there wasn't enough room in the sleigh. Santa, ever prepared, had a plan. He sprinkled some magic dust, and with a wave of his hand, two more sleighs appeared—one for Hope, who would drive with the deer and the bear, and another for Annoying, who would ride with the stork and the flamingos. Santa then covered their coats with a special magical shield to protect them from the cold weather, ensuring the drivers stayed warm and safe.

Together, they all set off into the starry night, ready to deliver Christmas gifts to boys and girls all over the world. The jingling of sleigh bells and the laughter of their new team echoed through the skies, spreading joy wherever they went.

53

In the end, everyone who had once hated Hope came to love and admire her for everything she had done. She forgave them all, gave each one a gift, and said, "Don't judge someone by how they look. Give them a chance and just listen; you'll learn to like them."
And so, with hearts full of joy and the spirit of Christmas guiding them, they embarked on a magical journey to spread happiness and cheer to all.

AUTHOR'S NOTE

On My Way to Find Christmas is a story about kindness, acceptance, and celebrating what makes us unique. Hope, the zebra, teaches us that being different is a gift and that true beauty lies in embracing who we are. Through her journey, she discovers the magic of friendship and the true spirit of Christmas.

May this story remind you to be kind, cherish your uniqueness, and spread love this holiday season.

55